Sound

by Ann J. Jacobs

PEARSON
Scott
Foresman

What is sound?

Look at the band.
You can see lots of instruments.
Each one makes a sound when it is played.

Sound is made when something vibrates.
Vibrate means to move quickly back
and forth.
This flute makes the air vibrate, which
makes sound.

Loudness

You can use loudness to tell about a sound. **Loudness** is how loud or soft a sound is.

How can you make a loud sound?
Bang on a drum!
What else makes a loud sound?

Some sounds are soft.
The leaves fall softly.
The kitten walks softly.

Tap a drum lightly.
It makes a soft sound.
What else makes soft sounds?

What is pitch?

Pitch means how high or low a sound is. Things that vibrate fast have a high pitch. Things that vibrate slowly have a low pitch.

Do you think this violin has a low or high pitch?
It can have a high pitch when the strings vibrate fast.
It can have a lower pitch when the strings vibrate slowly.

Find out more about pitch.
Blow across the top of a bottle.
What happens to the air inside the bottle?

**Lots of air,
low pitch**

The air inside the bottle vibrates.
Bottles with a lot of air make a sound with
a low pitch.
Bottles with less air make a sound with
a high pitch.

**Little air,
high pitch**

Look at the bottles.
Which one makes the sound with the
highest pitch?

Which one makes the sound with the lowest pitch?

Animals make many kinds of sounds. Animal sounds can have a low or a high pitch.

The bullfrog makes sounds with a low pitch.
This bird makes sounds with a high pitch.

How does sound travel?

Sound goes through solids, liquids, and gases.
Sound moves fast through the air.

This lion lets out a roar.
The sound goes through the air.

This bird pecks at a tree.
The sound moves through the tree and
the air.

This dolphin clicks.
The sound moves through the water.

Sound moves faster through water than through air.
Sound moves the fastest through solids, such as wood.

How do some animals make sounds?

Animals make sounds in lots of ways.
A cricket uses its wings.
It rubs them together.
The wings vibrate and make a sound.
The sound is like running your fingers
on the teeth of a comb.

A rattlesnake shakes its tail.
Its tail works like maracas.

A lobster makes sounds.
It rubs its antenna on the side of its head.
Its antenna works like a violin.

What are some sounds around you?

There are sounds all around.
You might hear a fire truck.
You might hear children.
You might hear a fly.

Every day we hear sounds.
Just listen!

Glossary

loudness   how loud or soft a sound is

pitch   how high or low a sound is

vibrate   to move quickly back and forth

What did you learn?

1. How is sound made?

2. What is pitch?

3. **Writing** in Science   Sound moves through gases, liquids, and solids. In your own words write to give an example of each. Use words from the book as you write.

4. **Important Details** Crickets make sound. What are some important details about how they do this?

Science

Genre	Comprehension Skill	Text Features	Science Content
Nonfiction	Important Details	• Labels • Glossary	Sound

Scott Foresman Science 2.11

scottforesman.com

ISBN 0-328-13799-5

90000

9 780328 137992

Deserts

By Madeline Boskey

Vocabulary

animals

early

eyes

full

warm

water

Word count: 93